Animal Mothers
Atsushi Komori
Illustrated by Masayuki Yabuuchi

THE BODLEY HEAD
London · Sydney
Toronto

Mother Cat carries her kittens
in her soft mouth.

Mother Lion carries her cub in her mouth, too.

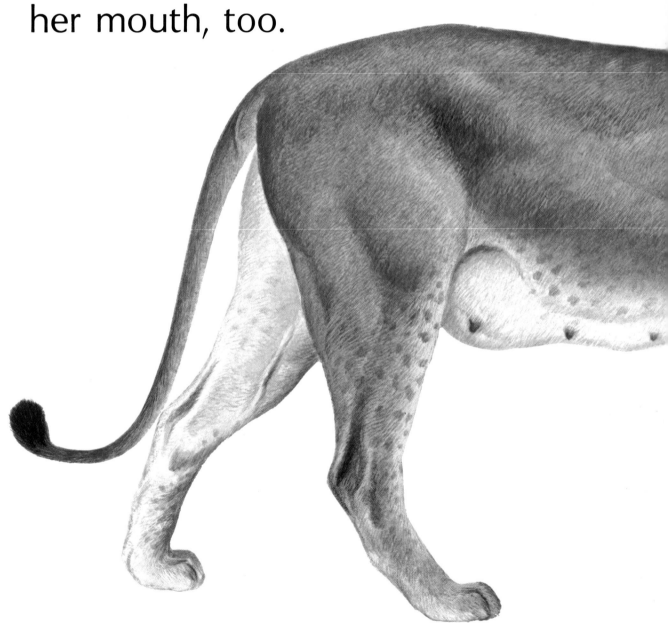

Mother Monkey's baby clings tightly to her stomach.

Mother Chimpanzee carries
her baby in her arms.

Mother Koala's cub
rides on her back.

Mother Sloth carries her baby on her stomach.

Mother Kangaroo carries
her joey in her pouch.

Mother Elephant gently
pushes her baby with her
trunk to make it run.

The Zebra foal runs along
behind its mother.

Baby Wild Boars follow their
mother all in a bunch.

Baby Hedgehogs follow their
mother in a nice straight line.